D1751291

Fall Is Here

People in Fall

by Sophie Geister-Jones

www.focusreaders.com

Copyright © 2021 by Focus Readers®, Lake Elmo, MN 55042. All rights reserved. No part of this book may be reproduced or utilized in any form or by any means without written permission from the publisher.

Focus Readers is distributed by North Star Editions:
sales@northstareditions.com | 888-417-0195

Produced for Focus Readers by Red Line Editorial.

Photographs ©: iStockphoto, cover, 1, 4, 7 (top), 9, 11, 13, 15, 16 (top left), 16 (top right), 16 (bottom left), 16 (bottom right); Shutterstock Images, 7 (bottom)

Library of Congress Cataloging-in-Publication Data
Names: Geister-Jones, Sophie, author.
Title: People in Fall / by Sophie Geister-Jones.
Description: Lake Elmo : Focus Readers, 2021. | Series: Fall is here | Includes index. | Audience: Grades K-1
Identifiers: LCCN 2020003748 (print) | LCCN 2020003749 (ebook) | ISBN 9781644933343 (Hardcover) | ISBN 9781644934104 (Paperback) | ISBN 9781644934869 (eBook) | ISBN 9781644935620 (PDF)
Subjects: LCSH: Outdoor recreation for children--Juvenile literature. | Autumn--Juvenile literature. | Halloween--Juvenile literature.
Classification: LCC GV191.63 .G45 2021 (print) | LCC GV191.63 (ebook) | DDC 796.083--dc23
LC record available at https://lccn.loc.gov/2020003748
LC ebook record available at https://lccn.loc.gov/2020003749

Printed in the United States of America
Mankato, MN
082020

About the Author

Sophie Geister-Jones is a writer who lives in Minnesota. She enjoys spending time with her family, reading, and taking too many pictures of her dog.

Table of Contents

Going Outside 5

Fall at Home 8

Trick or Treat 12

Glossary 16

Index 16

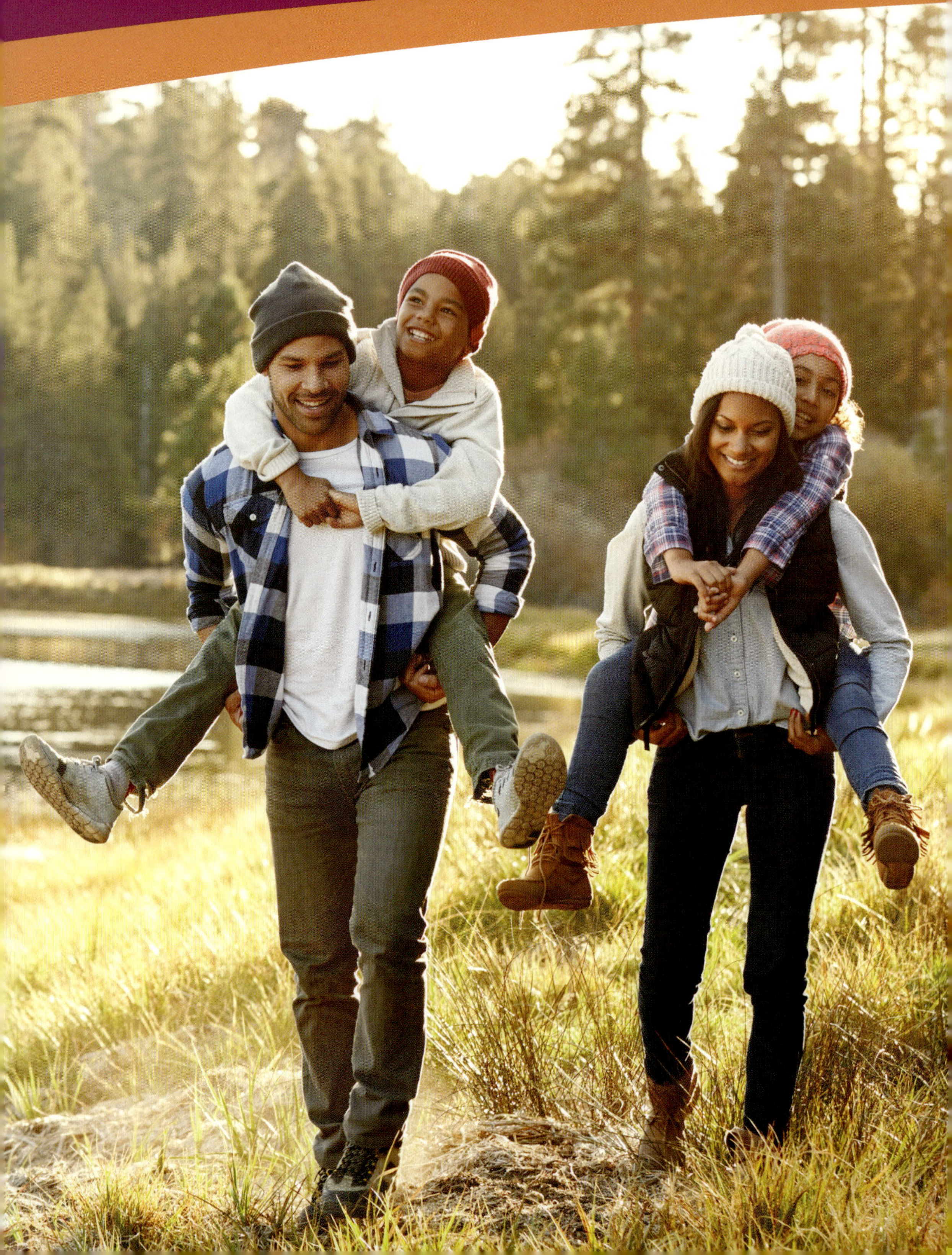

Going Outside

Fall is here.

We put on warm clothes.

We go outside.

We play in the **corn maze**.

We take a **tractor** ride.

corn maze

tractor

7

Fall at Home

We play outside.

We make leaf piles.

We jump in the piles.

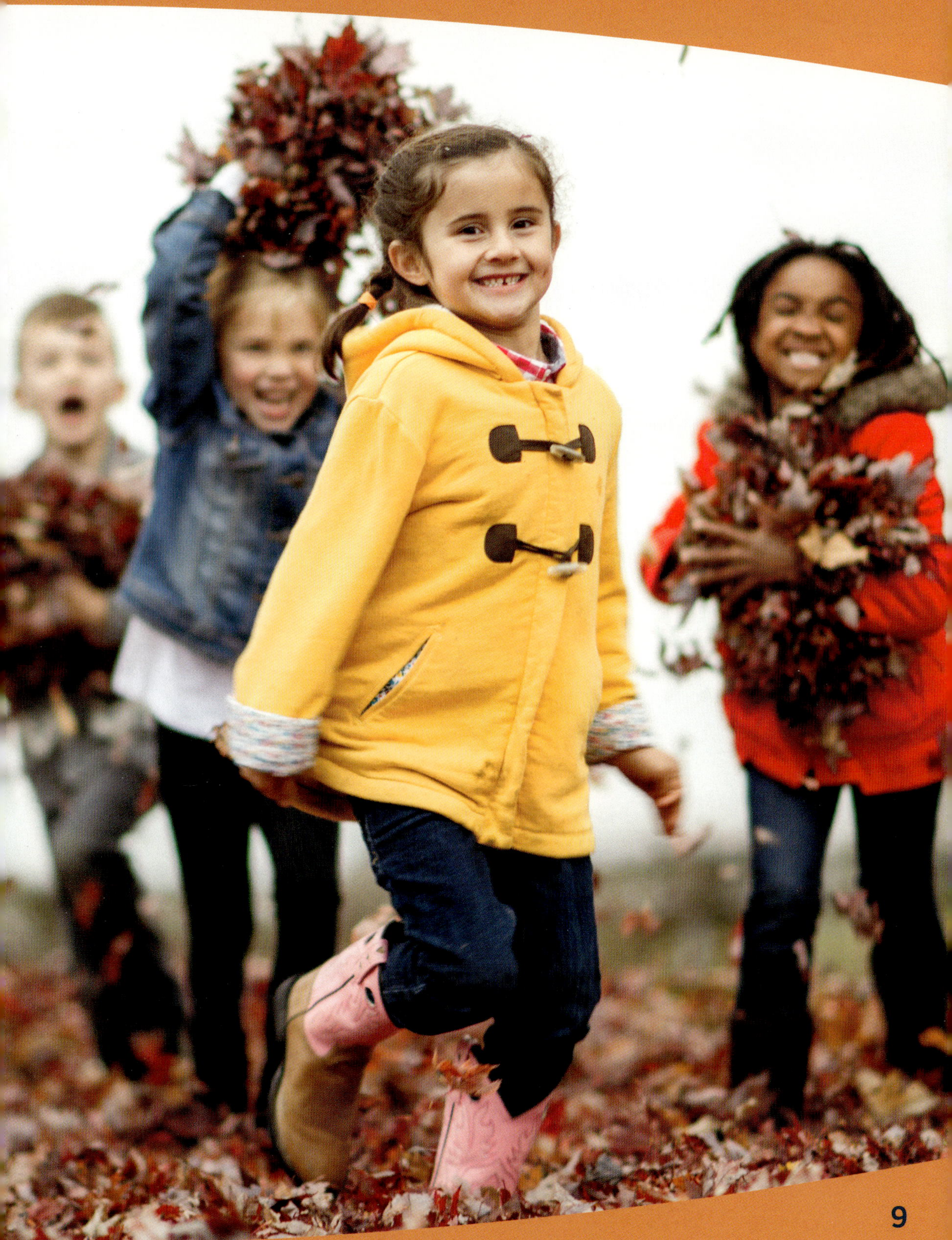

We spend time with family.

We paint **pumpkins**.

pumpkin

11

Trick or Treat

We go trick-or-treating.

We wear costumes.

costume

We get **candy**.

We share our candy.

We have fun in the fall.

candy

Glossary

candy

pumpkins

corn maze

tractor

Index

C
corn maze, 6

L
leaf piles, 8

P
pumpkins, 10

T
tractor, 6